COOKING WITH **OLIVE OIL**

COOKING WITH **OLIVE OIL**

THE ESSENCE OF THE MEDITERRANEAN: A CULINARY CELEBRATION OF THE OLIVE

BEVERLEY JOLLANDS

LORENZ BOOKS

This edition is published by Lorenz Books,
an imprint of Anness Publishing Ltd, Blaby Road, Wigston,
Leicestershire LE18 4SE; info@anness.com

www.lorenzbooks.com; www.annesspublishing.com

If you like the images in this book and would like to investigate using
them for publishing, promotions or advertising, please visit our website
www.practicalpictures.com for more information.

Publisher: Joanna Lorenz
Managing Editor: Helen Sudell
Senior Editor: Joanne Rippin
Location photography: Michelle Garrett
Styling and jacket design: Andrew Nash
Book design: Jester Designs
Editorial Reader: Hayley Kerr
Production controller: Claire Rae

© Anness Publishing Ltd 2012

NOTES
Bracketed terms are intended for American readers.
For all recipes, quantities are given in both metric and imperial
measures and, where appropriate, in standard cups and spoons.
Follow one set of measures, but not a mixture, because they
are not interchangeable.
Standard spoon and cup measures are level.
1 tsp = 5ml, 1 tbsp = 15ml, 1 cup = 250ml/8fl oz.
Australian standard tablespoons are 20ml. Australian readers should
use 3 tsp in place of 1 tbsp for measuring small quantities.
American pints are 16fl oz/2 cups. American readers should use 20fl
oz/2.5 cups in place of 1 pint when measuring liquids.
Electric oven temperatures in this book are for conventional ovens.
When using a fan oven, the temperature will probably need to be
reduced by about 10–20°C/20–40°F. Since ovens vary, you should
check with your manufacturer's instruction book for guidance.
Medium (US large) eggs are used unless otherwise stated.

Additional pictures supplied by: AKG (London)/Erich Lessing p8, 10, 11
left & 14 left; Ancient Art & Architecture/Mike Andrews p12; The
Bridgeman Art Library/British Museum p9 left, The Bridgeman Art
Library/Galleria degli Uffizi, Florence, *Athene and the Centaur* by
Botticelli p9 right; The Bridgeman Art Library/Biblioteque Nationale,
Paris p11 right; The Spanish Embassy p14 right.
Recipes supplied by: Jacqueline Clark, Joanna Farrow,
Brian Glover, Jeni Wright.
Recipes photographed by: Michelle Garrett and William Lingwood.

Contents

Introduction

The olive seems as central to the life and history of
the Mediterranean region as the sea. The sinuous,
shimmering trees, with their gnarled roots twined
into the stony soil, have sustained the civilizations
of the Mediterranean for more than 5000 years, and
their ability to survive and prosper in this unique
landscape is mirrored in the tenacity of the people
who tend them. The pungent, astringent taste of
olives evokes salt-laden wind and rocky, sun-
bleached hillsides. Laurence Durrell called it,
"A taste older than meat or wine, a taste as old as
cold water. Only the sea itself seems as ancient a
part of the region as the olive and its oil."
While olives now flourish in many parts of the
world, including California, South Africa and
Australia, the ancient roots of olive culture belong
to the Mediterranean, and all its varied cuisines
share the flavour of fragrant, fruity, luscious olive
oil. And since it is not only delicious but also very
good for us, there is every reason to seek out the
best of the lovely, traditional recipes that make the
most of olive oil's inimitable qualities.

The History of the Olive

The olive tree, *Olea europaea*, is one of the oldest cultivated species in the world. Its cultivation predates the written word, but seems to have begun in Iran and Syria, spreading from there to Palestine and the eastern Mediterranean. There are numerous Biblical references to the tree and its fruit, and a rich mythology surrounds its mysterious origins.

The olive in ancient times

Wall paintings and commercial records show that olives grew in ancient Egypt, and offerings of olive branches – such as those found in the tomb of Tutankhamun – accompanied the dead. The Egyptians used olive oil extensively, for cooking and lighting, in medicine and ritual. They ate the olives they grew, but for the highest quality oil they depended on imports from Palestine, Syria and Crete. The Cretans were producing oil in the third millennium BC and it is possible that this profitable trade was the source of the great wealth of the Minoans. When the palace of King Minos at Knossos was excavated, hundreds of the giant storage jars known as pithoi were found in its storerooms. They would once have been filled with olive oil. Cretan ships carried oil around the eastern Mediterranean, but when the Phoenicians took over the trade around 1200 BC they voyaged much further, and the

▲ The cellars of the Minoan palace of Knossos in Crete, where vast earthenware jars, or pithoi, were used to store olive oil.

▲ The harvesting methods shown on this Athenian amphora, decorated around 520 BC, are still in common use today.

taste for olive oil spread west along their trading routes into Italy, France, Spain, and as far as Carthage on the north African coast.

By the 6th century BC, the Greeks had become major exporters of oil, and the olive's status was so high that olive groves were regarded as sacred. In a curious pre-figuring of the modern idea of "virgin" olive oil, only the chaste were allowed to look after the trees and harvest the crop, and this custom survived into the Middle Ages. The destruction of an olive tree became a capital offence in Athens. A burning olive branch was the symbolic torch for the Olympic Games, at which the victor was crowned

▲ The olive tree was said to have been the goddess Athene's gift to the Greeks, and Botticelli's painting of Athene and a centaur shows her wreathed in olive boughs.

with a garland cut from the sacred olive growing on the Acropolis. At the Panathenaic Games, held in honour of Athene, the athletes competed for amphorae decorated with paintings of the goddess and filled with olive oil.

▲ A fragment of relief excavated at ancient Hermopolis in Upper Egypt shows an olive branch and the sticks used for the harvest.

A spreading culture

The Romans loved to eat olives, and developed new methods of curing them, but their greatest contribution to oil production was the invention of the screw press. This enabled them to crush the fruit mechanically to extract the maximum amount of oil from the flesh, but could be set to avoid breaking the stones (pits) and contaminating the oil.

The expansion of the Roman Empire increased the demand for olive oil, and Romans planted trees or traded oil in all the lands they conquered, regarding those who ate animal fats rather than olive oil as barbarians. Olive groves flourished throughout Italy, in southern France and Spain, on all the islands of the Mediterranean and along the north African coast from Tripoli to Algeria.

The olive's ancient progress westwards is reflected in its names. The words "olive" and "oil" come from the Latin *oliva* and *oleum*, which are both derived from the earliest Greek word for olive, *elaiwa*. Meanwhile, across the Mediterranean, the Semitic word *zayt* was adopted in the Arabic countries of north Africa, and reached Spain via the invading Moors. Therefore the Spanish word for olive is *aceituna* and the word for oil is *aceite*, although holy oil – because of the influence of the Roman church – is called *oleo santo*.

Control of the profitable trade in olive oil was crucial to the maintenance of Roman power, and was just as important in the 14th century when Venice became the dominant maritime power throughout the Mediterranean. From the 16th century, as the European conquistadors subdued and colonized the New World, olive saplings accompanied missionaries and immigrants on their voyages. Olive cultivation has gradually spread wherever the climate has proved suitable: to California, Chile and Argentina, China, Japan, New Zealand, southern Africa and Australia.

In recent years, the demand for olive oil has exploded in countries that used to disregard it. In the USA, for instance, consumption rose 2000 per cent

▲ The backbreaking business of picking olives up from the ground around the trees is shown in this detail, representing autumn, from a 2nd-century Roman floor mosaic.

between 1980–85, and it continues to increase by about 10 per cent each year. Today there are more than 800 million olive trees, but still about 90 per cent of them grow in their ancient home around the Mediterranean, and many olives are still grown, harvested and processed using techniques that the ancient Greeks and Romans would have recognized.

▶ An Italian olive oil merchant calls on two of his customers to replenish their supplies in this 14th-century illustration.

Olive Myths and Traditions

Wedded to human civilization for thousands of years, the olive has come to stand for many of life's positive aspects. Its origins are wreathed with myth. Some legends associate it with Adam and the Garden of Eden, but the most famous story of its birth links it with the foundation of Athens.

The tree of civilization

The gods Athene and Poseidon were rivals for patronage of the great city built around the Acropolis, and Zeus, the father of the gods, decreed that the winner would be the one who offered the most useful gift to the people: Poseidon created the horse, a symbol of mobility and war, but Athene produced the olive tree, an emblem of peace and stability, and won the contest. Acropos, the legendary founder of the city, was said to have been taught how to extract oil by Aristeus, the god of husbandry and son of Apollo, the sun god.

The sacred "City Olive" was planted on the Acropolis (there is still an olive tree there today), and the story of Athene's gift was recorded in marble on the frieze of the Parthenon. In 480 BC the Acropolis was burned down by the invading Persians, but the tree immediately sprouted again to become an emblem of hope, resurrection and permanence. Homer's wandering hero Odysseus built his marriage bed using a living olive tree as one of its posts: this

▲ The tree that grows by the portico of the Erechtheion on the Acropolis may well be descended from the "City Olive" of Athens.

made it immovable and permanent, as was his marriage. On the birth of a son in Athens, an olive wreath was hung on the front door.

The olive's long life has made it a symbol of civilization because it guarantees a settled future. The foundation of Rome was linked to it through the legend that Romulus and Remus were born under an olive tree. Olive groves literally root a family in its home, representing constancy and continuity, and eminent old trees are treated like family members, credited with individual characteristics and given pet names. Because the olive is not a wild plant, it needs human skill to help it flourish; in return it bestows riches on its "family".

Peace and honour

Greeks sometimes describe their friends as people they share bread and olives with, and everywhere the olive is recognized as a symbol of peace. Noah's dove, returning to the ark, carried an olive branch as a token of forgiveness, medieval heralds carried them

▲ Wreaths made of olive branches are seen as symbolizing forgiveness and peace.

to ensure their safety in enemy territory, and olive branches are part of the design on the United Nations flag.

In the ancient world anointing with oil was a general sign of respect for both the living and the dead; guests would be offered oil for their feet on arrival and on leaving. The Judaeo-Christian tradition continued the practice of anointing monarchs and priests – the words "Christ" and "Messiah" mean "anointed". Sacred monuments are also honoured with oil: libations of oil have been poured over the sacred Omphalos stone at Delphi, the Ka'aba in Mecca and the Jewish Ark of the Covenant, and Christian churches are consecrated using holy oil. And holy oil is olive oil.

▲ Libations of oil have been used in worship in many religions, and as a mark of respect for visitors too.

Oiling the Wheels of Life

In olive-growing areas, the trees rule more than just the eating habits of the people. It's easy to see why those who cultivate olives become so devoted to the them, since this multi-purpose tree not only earns them their living but has traditionally supplied so many of their needs.

Living with the olive

Olive oil was once an important light source all over the Mediterranean. The Phoenicians taught the Greeks how to do this, showing them how to make little clay lamps to hold the oil. It is still used for votive and sanctuary lamps that need to burn

▲ These two terracotta lamps, found in Jerusalem, were made around 2100 BC. The four spouts were used as rests for the wicks.

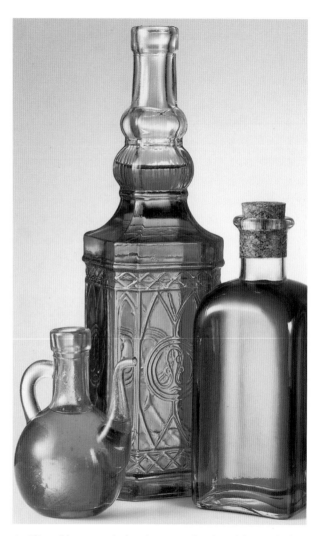

▲ Olive oil has a particular viscous quality that makes it ideal as a lubricant, and it was used to keep many materials supple.

continually, because it smokes very little. As a lubricant, olive oil also has many uses. It was traditionally used to dress wool to stop the fibres breaking during spinning; it stops metal rusting and keeps leather supple. Ancient marble statues were kept well-oiled to stop them cracking in hot weather, and it has also been used to polish diamonds.

The wood of the olive tree has a close grain that makes it very suitable for carving and turning, to make high-quality furniture, boxes and bowls. Olive stones and skins are either used as fuel or turned into fertilizer for the trees. The bitter substance in the fruit, called oleuropein, which has to be separated from the oil during processing, was collected by the ancient Romans for use as a weedkiller and pesticide.

Scents and soaps

For special occasions, ancient Egyptians wore on their heads cones of scented ointment, made with olive oil, which gradually melted and ran down over their bodies, and scented oils for the hair and skin were popular all over the Mediterranean. Olive oil was also used to clean the skin until the invention of soap provided an alternative method.

The ancient Gauls made soap from animal fats and potash, and the growing trade centred on Marseilles, from where the new product was exported around the Roman world. However, the Castilians in Spain developed a luxury soap made from olive oil and in the eighth century the Marseilles soap-makers adopted their method. A French law of 1668, still in force, stipulated that only soap made exclusively with olive oil could be called savon de Marseille. A handful of manufacturers in the area still make the traditional product, claimed to be the finest soap in the world.

▼ Traditional Marseilles soap, with the subtle colours and scents of olive oil and herbs, is stamped to guarantee its quality.

The Olive Tree

An olive tree can live for centuries, and even if the original growth is cut down, new shoots will emerge from the root. Left to itself, the tree will grow to 15m (50ft), but is kept smaller by pruning. It is an evergreen related to the privet, lilac, jasmine and oleander, but the species is not found growing wild, implying that its early growers developed it by careful selection, yet how and where they did so remains a mystery. It does have a wild relative called the oleaster, or wild olive, which is sometimes used as a rootstock for olive grafts, but this is not thought to be its ancestor. There are over 150 cultivated varieties, which are propagated from cuttings.

The olive's year

Tiny flowers appear in late spring, and dry weather is needed to ensure good fertilization, as rain can knock the blossoms off the trees. The fruits are green at first, gradually ripening to black. They reach their maximum oil content when fully ripe, at least six months after the blossom, but the finest oil is produced from fruit that is just beginning to ripen.

In autumn the trees are pruned quite rigorously: according to an Italian proverb, an olive tree needs a sage at its feet and a fool at its head. The top growth is thinned to expose the fruit to the sun and air, and the suckers are removed. Pruning helps to concentrate the tree's energy in the new shoots.

▲ Mature olive trees soak up the sun on an Italian hillside. The ground around them is cleared to ensure the most plentiful crop.

▲ These ancient Greek olives, rigorously pruned, seem as old and gnarled as the rocks amongst which they are growing.

Growing conditions

The olive's requirements are exactly supplied by the Mediterranean soil and climate in the hilly regions: free-draining, limy soil, a dry spring to ensure good fertilization, and a long, hot summer. A little winter cold is also essential to set the fruit, and the trees can survive some frost, down to about −11°C (12°F), if they have perfect drainage.

While long roots and small leaves enable olives to cope well with drought, the yield is greater if the trees are watered, pruned and fertilized, and the ground weeded to eliminate competition for water.

Olives in the garden

If you can supply the conditions the olive needs, it makes an exciting and beautiful specimen tree, especially grown alongside other Mediterranean plants. As most varieties are self-pollinating, you need only one tree to produce home-grown olives. It needs a sunny sheltered site, and a really gritty soil to ensure that its roots are not left sitting in winter damp. In cold areas it can be grown in a container and given some winter protection.

▲ The Mediterranean olive tree grows alongside the region's human communities: it is not found in the wild.

The Olive Harvest

Harvesting begins in autumn and may continue until the following spring, as the timing depends on the area and whether the fruit is for eating or for oil. In wine-growing areas, the olive harvest traditionally follows the grape harvest – in Provence, for instance, it is traditional to start picking on 15 November.

Though the harvest is labour-intensive, it comes at a relatively quiet time of year – in the Mediterranean, this is after most tourists have gone home. Traditionally, the picking and pressing was done by sailors home from sea for the winter, and many people still go home to help out – Greek civil servants are officially allowed time off work to pick

▲ In this Moroccan grove, the trees have grown to their natural height. The pickers climb them, or use poles to beat the branches.

their olives. The traditional olive harvest is a social event, like the grape harvest, with the whole village turning out to help pick each other's crop.

Picking the olives

Even in these days of highly industrialized farming, for the finest olive oil the fruit is still carefully picked by hand from a ladder. The pickers will return to the trees repeatedly to pick only the ripe fruit. The olives are then dropped gently into nets that are slung from the trees to avoid bruising them, as damaged fruit starts to deteriorate very quickly.

▲ The harvest is a communal activity and the fruit needs to be sorted speedily to preserve its quality, as here in Morocco.

Another time-honoured method is to hit the branches with long poles, so that the ripe fruit falls to the ground where large nets are spread under the trees. This tends to knock down branches as well as fruit, making it a rather indiscriminate method of thinning, but the rough treatment was long thought to be good for the trees, and farmers used to encourage it by giving the pickers the wood that came down to take home for fuel.

On steep hillsides, there is little alternative to the traditional methods. Shaking machines can be used for more accessible trees, but the olives still have to be picked up from the ground. This has to be done quickly for the best quality olive oil: once the olives are piled up together they start to heat up and ferment, which raises their acidity. The average yield from a mature tree is 15–20kg (33–44lb), which will produce 3–4 litres (5–7 pints) of oil.

The olive mill

Once all the olives are picked, they are taken to the mill for pressing. During the harvest, pressing goes on day and night to avoid keeping the olives waiting. If they do have to wait, they are spread out thinly and kept cool, but ideally the time between harvesting and pressing should not exceed two days. The mill may be on the farm itself, or may belong to a co-operative. Small-scale olive growers can have their crop pressed in a local mill for their own use, or to sell, or they may sell the crop on to a large producer.

Washing the olives gets rid of the leaves and other rubbish, then the flesh is crushed to a paste. The many small mills that produce the finest cold-pressed oils still crush the olives using traditional millstones. The paste, already oozing and dripping, is then spread on woven hemp mats and stacked between metal discs that are placed in a hydraulic press to extract the oil.

The oil is left to settle, then decanted off the vegetable water, which takes with it the bitter, toxic oleuropein. Finally, most oil is filtered, possibly several times. Cotton is used for the very best oils, though alkaline earth is more usual as this helps to lower acidity. The result is fine-quality, cold-pressed olive oil, ready to use.

▲ These woven hemp mats are used in the process of extracting olive oil.

Pressings and Grades

Like wine, olive oil is infinitely variable, and learning to appreciate its different flavours can be just as satisfying as wine-tasting. The large producers blend their oils to achieve a consistent flavour, but the market for characterful oils from individual growers is expanding all the time. Variations depend on the country of origin, the soil, the variety of the olives used, the harvest and the method of pressing. The colour of oil depends on the ripeness of the olives used to make it, and can range from deep green to light gold. It is not only an indicator of quality.

Unlike wine, olive oil doesn't improve with age, though it does keep well in good conditions (away from light and heat). It's at its best during the year following pressing.

The first pressing

The very highest quality oil is the small amount that oozes out of the olive paste without any added pressure. The Spanish call this *flor del aceite*, or "flower of the oil".

Traditional presses extract only about half the oil from the paste using pressure alone: this is the "first pressing", which may also be labelled "cold pressed". Modern presses and centrifuges are able to extract more oil without using heat. After the cold pressing, heat can be used to extract more oil from the paste, but the flavour will be degraded.

▲ Using technology that was familiar in Roman times, ripe black olives are gently crushed in a mill driven by mule-power.

Virgin oils

Oils produced without the use of heat or additional chemicals are classified according to their level of acidity – the proportion of oleic acid in the oil. The lowest acidity gives the best flavour. These classifications are regulated by the International Olive Oil Council.

- Extra virgin: acidity less than 1 per cent (the best oils have less than 0.5 per cent acidity)

- Fine virgin: acidity less than 1.5 per cent
- Semi-fine virgin: acidity less than 3 per cent

Refined oils

Oils produced from second and subsequent pressings, using steam and solvents, have to be refined to lower their acidity and neutralize flavour. The flavour may then be improved by adding a small proportion of extra virgin oil. The result is called "pure olive oil" or simply "olive oil".

Olive residue (pomace) oil, a crude oil chemically extracted from the remaining olive paste, may be further refined for sale as olive oil (or for uses such as packing canned fish), or used industrially for treating wool and making soap and other toiletries.

▶ The different types of olive oil are easily recognized by colour; the finest grade virgin olive oil has a distinctive green shade.

Tasting oil

If you assemble a number of distinctive olive oils you can try a comparative tasting in the same way as you would taste wine. Pour each oil into a glass. Warm it in your hands and swirl it around the glass, then inhale to test the aroma. Take a sip and note the flavours, which can range from fruity, mellow or grassy to peppery and pleasantly bitter. The oil should not taste fatty in the mouth, or acid in the throat. Cleanse your palate between oils by eating a slice of apple.

The Major Oil Producers

Although olives now grow all round the world, the countries of the Mediterranean still produce most of the world's oil. They also use the most, and consumption is highest of all in Greece, where the average person gets through over 20 litres (35 pints) of olive oil a year.

Spain

As the largest producer, with over 300 million trees, Spain accounts for 35 per cent of the world's olive oil. Much of this is exported in bulk, often to Italy where it is blended with Italian oil. But there are also wonderful single estate oils, and Spain was the first country to establish a Denominacion de Origen for its sweet, smooth virgin olive oils. The major brands of blended oils are Ybarra and Carbonell.

Italy

Olives have been grown in Italy since around the 6th century BC. Apulia in the south has the most, while the rich, fruity green oils of Tuscany are often produced as an additional crop by wine growers. Italy is the second largest producer in the world, but the Italians themselves consume more oil than they produce – 11 litres (19 pints) per person each year – and Italian law allows the producers to import oil for blending and bottling without stating its original source. So, while some of the finest single estate oils

▲ The verdant olive groves of Italy produce lush, deep green oils with flavours that characterize the country's cuisine.

come from Italy, most of the blended oil labelled "bottled in Italy" on the supermarket shelf is actually Spanish, Greek or Tunisian in origin. Major Italian brands include Berio, Sasso and Bertolli.

Greece

The 137 million olive trees of Greece are a mainstay of the nation's economy, in a land where few other crops will grow. The value of land is still sometimes based on the number of olive trees growing on it, and in Crete over 60 per cent of the cultivated land is planted with olives. Three-quarters of Greece's total production is extra virgin oil – much of it made from the Kalamata olive, deep green, strong and fruity. Iliada and Karyatis are leading brands.

France

Provence is the main oil-producing region, but many of the old olive groves are now being replaced by more profitable vines. All Provençal oil is made by small-scale growers and little is exported.

America

The Mission variety of olive was brought to California by Franciscan missionaries in the 18th century. Its small fruits are slow to fall from the tree so they can be left until they are fully ripe, producing a sweet, golden oil. California produces a tiny proportion of the world's oil, but the industry is growing as demand increases.

The rest of the world

Tunisia is a significant producer of oil, but exports most of it in bulk to Italy for blending and bottling. Other oil-producing countries include Portugal, where port producers often grow olives as a secondary crop, Morocco, Algeria, Libya, Turkey, Israel, Jordan and Syria. Away from the Mediterranean, olives grow in South Africa, Argentina and Chile, Australia, Japan and China.

▲ The olive grove is an essential part of the landscape of Greece, and olive oil has always been central to the Greek economy.

The Mediterranean Diet

Crete has the highest consumption of olive oil per head in the world: it also has the lowest death rate from cardiovascular disease and the highest proportion of centenarians – a persuasive argument for the merits of the style of eating that is now described as "the Mediterranean diet".

Because the Mediterranean region offers little pasture for raising animals, but a lot of sun and sea, its people have traditionally lived on quantities of ripe fruit, herbs, seafood and bread, with relatively little meat and dairy produce. And they use a lot of olive oil.

Limiting the amount of fat we eat is a modern preoccupation, but some fat is an essential part of a

▲ The simplest way to enjoy truly great olive oil is to dunk a piece of good bread into it – a traditional Mediterranean snack.

balanced diet. We need to know not only how much we are eating, but what kind. Fats are defined by the chemical bonds between their carbon groups:

- Saturated fats have a simple bond and are found in meat and dairy produce – butter, lard and other animal fat.
- Unsaturated fats have a double bond and are found in vegetable oils. There are two kinds:
- Polyunsaturated fatty acids (with several double bonds) such as linoleic and linolenic acid – these are high in sunflower and corn oils.
- Monounsaturated fatty acids (with one double bond) such as oleic acid, which is highest in olive oil (with up to 80 per cent).

▲ Sun-ripened fruits, herbs and bread, with relatively little dairy produce, are staple elements of the healthy Mediterranean diet.

Cholesterol

It's well known that eating too much saturated fat increases the amount of cholesterol deposited in the blood vessels. Eating olive oil not only avoids this build-up but can actually reduce it.

There are two types of cholesterol. Low density lipoproteins (LDL) transport and deposit cholesterol in the blood vessels – these increase with a high intake of saturated fat. High density lipoproteins (HDL) also transport cholesterol, but they take it to the liver for elimination. Eating unsaturated fats reduces this "good" cholesterol along with the bad, but eating monounsaturated fat – olive oil – increases it, reducing cholesterol levels in the body.

Other health benefits

Taking olive oil has been recommended for centuries to aid digestion and reduce the effects of alcohol. Modern studies are still adding to an impressive list of the ways in which eating it regularly can improve your health.

Olive remedies

• *An infusion of olive leaves is said to reduce hypertension and heart conditions, and is a diuretic. (The leaves contain salicylic acid, the active constituent of aspirin.)*

• *The hardened sap of the tree, known as "Lucca gum" can be chewed to relieve toothache.*

▲ Many advocates of the health benefits of olive oil recommend a daily dose of a couple of spoonfuls to help lower cholesterol.

• It reduces gastric acidity, and helps to protect against ulcers.
• It helps prevent constipation, and may reduce the risk of colon cancer.
• It stimulates bile secretion and reduces the risk of gallstones.
• The antioxidants in extra virgin oil may help to reduce blood pressure.
• During pregnancy, oleic acid and Vitamin E aid the development of the baby's bones, brain and nervous system.
• It relieves wear and tear on the brain and other organs, reducing the effects of aging.
• It speeds the healing of wounds.

Oil for Beauty and Wellbeing

The Greek philosopher Democritus had a simple recipe for health: honey on the inside and oil on the outside. The ancient Greeks and Romans certainly knew that olive oil was good for the skin, and oiled their skin after baths, before meals, before and after exercise and before and after journeys.

Olive oil has been used for centuries to ease tired muscles, soften rough skin and soothe abrasions. It's also a traditional conditioning treatment for the hair, giving it body and shine.

Facial mask for dry skin

1 egg yolk
15ml (1 tbsp) olive oil
lemon juice

Beat the egg yolk and add the olive oil gradually. Add a few drops of lemon juice. Smooth on to your face and leave until dry, then rinse off.

Cleansing mask for blackheads

30ml (2 tbsp) oatmeal
30ml (2 tbsp) yogurt
15ml (1 tbsp) lemon juice
15ml (1 tbsp) olive oil

Mix the ingredients to a paste and spread on the face. Leave for 10 minutes then rinse off with cool water.

Dry hair conditioning treatment

1 egg yolk
120ml (4fl oz/$\frac{1}{2}$ cup) olive oil
2 drops lavender essential oil

Beat the egg yolk and gradually add the olive oil, then the essential oil. Massage the mixture into your hair and wrap a hot, damp towel around it. Leave for at least an hour before shampooing and rinsing thoroughly.

Honey conditioner

45ml (3 tbsp) clear honey

120ml (4fl oz/$1/_2$ cup) olive oil

2 drops rosemary essential oil

15ml (1 tbsp) cider vinegar

Mix the honey with the olive oil and add the rosemary essential oil. Massage the mixture into your hair and wrap a hot, damp towel around it. Leave for at least an hour before shampooing and rinsing thoroughly, adding the cider vinegar to the water for the final rinse to make the hair shine.

Cold cream

The Greek physician Galen is said to have invented cold cream in the 2nd century AD. He did this by melting one part wax and adding three parts olive oil, then blending in as much water as the mixture would hold.

Olive oil body scrub

120ml (4fl oz/$1/_2$cup) olive oil

30ml (2 tbsp) sea salt

Mix the ingredients together. Take a shower and, while your skin is still wet, rub the mixture over your body (avoiding any broken skin). Rinse off thoroughly in the shower.

Quick beauty tips

- Massage the skin with a mixture of olive oil and lemon juice to prevent wrinkles.
- Rub a little olive oil into your fingernails each night before you go to bed, to stop them chipping and flaking.
- For a super-rich face mask, mix olive oil and a mashed avocado and leave on the face for 15–20 minutes.
- To combat spots, add a drop of lavender essential oil to a little olive oil and apply to the problem area.

Culinary Uses

Whether you drizzle it over salads and bread or use it in cooking, olive oil is a magical ingredient. It is the only oil that is edible as soon as it emerges from the press, with no further processing. Olive oils vary widely in quality, flavour and aroma, and the different grades are suitable for different purposes.

▲ Keep a selection of grades and pressings of olive oil in your kitchen so that you are able to use the right oil for each purpose.

Dressing and flavouring

When used in salad dressings, the flavour of the olive oil needs to suit the ingredients of the dish. Peppery extra virgin oil adds its powerful personality to a robust green or potato salad, but a lighter, sweeter style suits more delicate ingredients. Combine oil with wine, sherry or cider vinegar, or use vinegar flavoured with herbs, chilli or fruit. Lemon juice adds a sharper flavour and a lively tang.

Trickle a high-quality oil over a hot dish just before you eat it, or use it to make a very simple pasta sauce in which the olive oil's flavour is dominant. Added to a dish at the end of cooking, it will calm sharp flavours and give a sauce extra richness.

Marinades

Used in marinades, olive oil harmonizes the other flavours and helps the ingredients to penetrate and tenderize the food. Choose an oil-based marinade for lean meat, poultry or white fish, which may dry out during cooking. If the food is to be griddled or barbecued, brush the marinade over it during cooking to add extra flavour and keep it moist.

Frying

Pure olive oil has a high smoke-point, so is suitable for deep-frying. When very hot, it seals the surface of the food, preventing the absorption of too much oil and preserving the flavours. It is wonderful for frying fish. Extra virgin oil has a lower smoke-point, and is anyway too expensive to use in large quantities for deep-frying, but is ideal for sautéing meat and sweating vegetables.

Roasting

Rub oil over meat and poultry before roasting and baste during cooking to produce delicious crisp skin on chicken, and perfect crackling on pork. Toss vegetables in plenty of olive oil before roasting them in a very hot oven.

Baking

Olive oil gives bread a distinctive flavour and produces a soft, moist dough that rises well. It also improves the keeping quality of the bread.

Classic vinaigrette

30ml/2 tbsp vinegar
10ml/2 tsp Dijon mustard
90ml/6 tbsp olive oil
salt and ground black pepper

Put the vinegar in a bowl and add the mustard, salt and pepper. Whisk to combine. Slowly drizzle in the oil, whisking constantly, until the vinaigrette is smooth and well blended. Check the seasoning and adjust if necessary.

▲ Traditional cans protect the oil from light and their narrow spouts allow you to pour it in a fine, controllable stream.

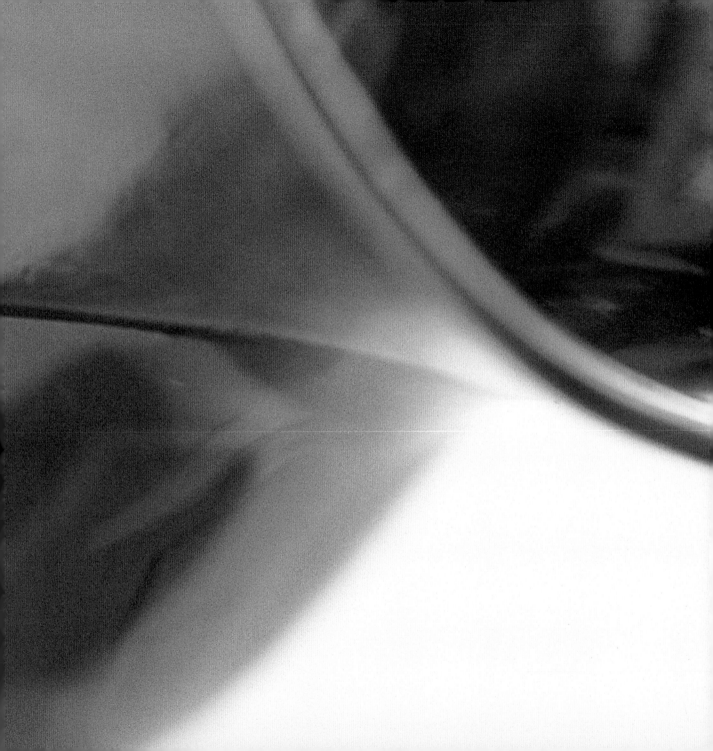

Cooking with Olive Oil

Just as the olive tree is rooted into the fabric of Mediterranean life, so is olive oil a fundamental part of the cooking traditions of Italy, Spain and Greece. The oil is used not only as a cooking medium, for frying or roasting, but as a flavour and ingredient in its own right. Olive oil is drizzled over toasted bread for breakfast in Spain, it would be unthinkable to have any kind of salad without a dressing of olive oil, or a cooked vegetable without a quick slug of olive oil added before serving. It is even eaten as a tapas or appetizer with chunks of crusty bread dipped into it. The selection of recipes that follow show the scope that olive oil has as a main ingredient, in dishes that demonstrate its satisfying depth of richness and flavour.

DRIZZLES AND NIBBLES

Extra virgin oils with rich, deep flavours are best savoured raw. Use them to dress salads
and lightly cooked vegetables, or drizzle them over dips. Olive oil is the key ingredient in many classic
Mediterranean dips and sauces, to go with nibbles to eat with drinks or as a relaxed start to a meal. Chunks
of crusty bread dunked into a bowl of fruity oil make the simplest appetizer of all.

Garlic oil

*Flavouring olive oil with garlic is a wonderful way to preserve the tastes of
summer, as it can be stored in a cool, dry place for 3–6 months.*

several large whole cloves of garlic
600ml/1 pint/2^1/$_2$ cups light olive oil

1 Peel the whole garlic cloves. Push the cloves into clean, dry bottles. If the
cloves are too large for the neck of the bottle, cut them in half lengthways.

2 Fill the bottles to the top with the olive oil, and cork. Leave for 2 weeks to
infuse (steep). Check the flavour and if it is as strong as you want it to be,
remove the cloves by straining the oil through a muslin-lined sieve and
pouring into clean bottles.

Variations

• *Garlic-infused oil: for a gentler garlic taste, peel several cloves of
garlic, put into a small pan and just cover with olive oil. Poach very
gently for about 25 minutes. Leave to cool, then strain out the garlic
before bottling the oil.*
• *Spiced herb oils: add spiciness with cinnamon sticks, dried chillies,
whole cloves, cardamom pods, coriander seeds or peppercorns.*
• *Lemon oil: add lemon zest to any of the spice oils for an added twist.*

Basil oil

This has a delicious Mediterranean flavour. If you wish, use oil that has already been infused with garlic.

about 15g/¹/₂oz/¹/₂ cup basil leaves
450ml/³/₄ pint/scant 2 cups olive oil

1 Bruise the basil leaves lightly using a mortar and pestle, then stir in a little of the oil. Gently combine the oil and basil.

2 Pour the mixture into a clean, dry bottle and top up with the rest of the oil. Cover and store in a cool place for 2–3 weeks.

3 Strain the oil through a muslin-lined sieve, leaving it to drip through without squeezing the leaves. Pour into a clean bottle.

Warning

Oils containing fresh herbs can grow harmful moulds. To protect against this, remove the herbs once they have flavoured the oil, or use dried.

Tapas of almonds, olives and marinated cheese

Serves 6–8

These three simple dishes create a delicious Spanish medley to serve with an aperitif, the ideal accompaniment to chilled dry sherry.

For the marinated olives:
2.5ml/$\frac{1}{2}$ tsp coriander seeds
2.5ml/$\frac{1}{2}$ tsp fennel seeds
5ml/1 tsp chopped fresh rosemary
10ml/2 tsp chopped fresh parsley
2 garlic cloves, crushed
15ml/1 tbsp sherry vinegar
30ml/2 tbsp olive oil
225g/8oz/1$\frac{1}{3}$ cup mixed olives

For the marinated cheese:
150g/5oz manchego cheese
90ml/6 tbsp olive oil
15ml/1 tbsp white wine vinegar
5ml/1 tsp black peppercorns
1 garlic clove, sliced
3 sprigs of fresh tarragon or thyme

For the salted almonds:
1.5ml/$\frac{1}{4}$ tsp cayenne pepper
30ml/2 tbsp sea salt
60ml/4 tbsp olive oil
200g/7oz/1$\frac{3}{4}$ cups blanched almonds

1 To make the marinated olives, crush the coriander and fennel seeds with a mortar and pestle. Mix with the rosemary, parsley, garlic, vinegar and oil and pour over the olives. Cover and chill for up to 1 week.

2 To make the marinated cheese, cut the manchego cheese into bite-size pieces, leaving the rind on. Mix the other ingredients and pour them over the cheese. Cover and chill for up to 3 days.

3 To make the salted almonds, mix the cayenne and salt in a bowl. Heat the oil in a frying pan and fry the almonds, stirring, until golden. Tip the nuts into the salt mixture and toss. Leave to cool, then store in an airtight container.

Tapenade and herb aioli with summer vegetables

Serves 6

A platter of vegetables served with a choice of interesting French sauces makes an appetizing first course for an informal meal.

For the tapenade:
175g/6oz/1¹/₂ cups pitted black olives
50g/2oz can anchovy fillets, drained
30m/¹/₂ tbsp capers
120ml/4fl oz/¹/₂ cup olive oil
finely grated rind of 1 lemon
15ml/1 tbsp brandy

For the herb aioli:
2 egg yolks
5ml/1 tsp Dijon mustard
10ml/2 tsp white wine vinegar
250ml/8fl oz/1 cup light olive oil
45ml/3 tbsp chopped mixed fresh herbs, such as chervil, parsley or tarragon
30ml/2 tbsp chopped watercress
5 garlic cloves, crushed

To serve:
2 red (bell) peppers, seeded and sliced
summer vegetables, such as new potatoes, beans, carrots and asparagus
quail's eggs

1 To make the tapenade, finely chop the olives, anchovies and capers and beat together with the oil, lemon rind and brandy. Blend in a little more oil if the mixture seems dry, and check the seasoning.

2 To make the aioli, beat together the egg yolks, mustard and vinegar. Gradually blend in the oil, a drop at a time, whisking well until the mixture is thick and smooth. Season with salt and pepper to taste. Stir in the herbs, watercress and garlic.

3 Brush the peppers with oil and grill (broil) until beginning to char. Boil the potatoes until just tender. Add the beans and carrots and cook for 1 minute. Add the asparagus and cook for a further 30 seconds, then drain. Boil the eggs for 2 minutes.

4 Put each sauce in a bowl, arrange all the vegetables, eggs and sauces on a large platter and garnish with fresh herbs. Serve at room temperature with coarse salt for sprinkling.

Hummus bi tahina

Serves 4–6

This classic purée, a creamy blend of chickpeas, sesame paste and olive oil, is eaten as part of a Turkish-style mezze or as a dip with vegetables.

150g/5oz/³/₄ cup dried chickpeas
juice of 2 lemons
2 garlic cloves, sliced
30ml/2 tbsp olive oil, plus extra for drizzling
pinch of cayenne pepper
150ml/¹/₄ pint/²/₃ cup tahini paste
salt and ground black pepper

1 Soak the chickpeas overnight in plenty of cold water. Drain, put in a pan and cover with fresh water. Bring to the boil and cook rapidly for 10 minutes, then simmer gently for about 1 hour, until soft. Drain.

2 Process the chickpeas in a food processor to a smooth purée. Add the lemon juice, garlic, oil, cayenne pepper and tahini and blend until creamy. Season with salt and pepper to taste. Transfer to a serving dish and drizzle with more olive oil.

Brandade de morue

Salt cod is popular in Spain and France, and is cooked in many different ways. This purée is made all over southern France.

1 Cover the drained fish with fresh water in a large pan. Cover, bring to the boil, and simmer for 8–10 minutes, until tender. Drain and flake.

2 Heat the oil until very hot. In a separate pan, scald the milk. Put the fish in a food processor, switch on and slowly add the oil, then the milk. Beat in the rest of the ingredients. Leave to cool, then transfer to a serving dish.

3 To make the croutes, heat the oil in a frying pan and fry the slices of bread until golden. Drain on kitchen paper, then rub both sides with garlic and serve with the brandade and olives.

Serves 6

675g/1¹/₂lb salt cod, soaked for 24 hours, changing the water several times, and then drained
300ml/¹/₂ pint/1¹/₄ cups olive oil
250ml/8fl oz/1 cup milk
1 garlic clove, crushed
grated nutmeg
lemon juice, to taste
white pepper

For the croutes:
50ml/2fl oz/¹/₄ cup olive oil
6 slices white bread, crusts removed, halved diagonally
1 garlic clove, halved

To serve:
a selection of green and black olives

Bagna cauda

Serves 4

This hot garlic dip comes from Piedmont in northern Italy, where it is traditionally eaten to celebrate the end of the grape harvest.

150ml/¹/₄ pint/²/₃ cup olive oil
5cm/2in sprig fresh rosemary
6 garlic cloves, finely chopped
50g/2oz can anchovy fillets, drained and chopped
90g/3 ¹/₂oz/7 tbsp unsalted (sweet) butter
ground black pepper

To serve:
a selection of vegetables, such as new potatoes, baby artichokes, cauliflower florets, fennel, celery, baby carrots, lightly cooked as necessary
crusty bread
large cooked prawns (shrimp)

1 Place the olive oil in a pan over a very low heat and add the rosemary and garlic. Allow the flavours to permeate the oil for about 5 minutes. Remove the rosemary and add the anchovies, mashing them into the oil.

2 When the anchovies have broken down completely, add the butter and whisk gently until it has melted. Add pepper to taste and pour into a flameproof dish. Surround with the prepared vegetables, bread and prawns and serve immediately, keeping hot over a spirit stove if possible.

Marinated baby aubergines with raisins and pine nuts

Serves 4

Make this recipe, which has an Italian influence, a day in advance to allow the sour and sweet flavours to develop, and serve as an appetizer.

12 baby aubergines, (eggplant) halved lengthways
250ml/8fl oz/1 cup olive oil
juice of 1 lemon
30ml/2 tbsp balsamic vinegar
3 cloves, 1 bay leaf
25g/1oz/$\frac{1}{3}$ cup pine nuts
25g/1oz/2 tbsp raisins
15ml/1 tbsp granulated sugar
large pinch dried chilli flakes or chilli powder
salt and ground black pepper

1 Preheat the grill (broiler) to high. Brush the aubergines with a little oil and grill (broil) for 10 minutes until slightly blackened, turning once.

2 To make the marinade, mix the remaining oil with the other ingredients. Place the hot aubergines in a non-metallic bowl and pour over the marinade. Leave to cool, turning the aubergines once or twice.

Tortilla

The olive oil is used in quantity here so that the potatoes almost boil rather than fry; this makes them wonderfully tender and flavoursome.

Serves 4

1 Heat the oil in a large non-stick frying pan. Cook the onions and potato gently, stirring from time to time, for about 20 minutes, until soft.

2 Beat the eggs in a large bowl. Remove the onion and potato from the pan with a slotted spoon and stir into the eggs, seasoning to taste.

3 Pour off some of the oil to leave about 60ml/4 tbsp in the pan, and re-heat. When very hot, add the egg mixture and cook for 2–3 minutes. Cover the pan with a plate and invert the omelette. Slide it back into the pan and cook for a further 5 minutes, until golden brown but still moist in the middle. Cut into wedges to serve.

300ml/^{1}/$_2$ pint/1^1/$_4$ cups olive oil
2 Spanish onions, sliced
3 large potatoes, peeled and sliced
6 eggs
salt and ground black pepper

Roasted pepper antipasto

Serves 6

Serve this beautifully coloured dish as an appetizer on its own or with Italian salamis and cold meats.

3 red (bell) peppers

2 yellow or orange (bell) peppers

2 green (bell) peppers

50g/2oz/$^1/_2$ cup sun-dried tomatoes in oil, drained

1 garlic clove

30ml/2 tbsp balsamic vinegar

75ml/5 tbsp olive oil

few drops of chilli sauce

4 canned artichoke hearts, drained and sliced

salt and ground black pepper

basil leaves, to garnish

1 Preheat the oven to 200°C/400°F/Gas 6. Place the peppers on a lightly oiled baking sheet and bake for about 45 minutes, until beginning to char. Cover with a cloth and leave to cool for 5 minutes.

2 Thinly slice the sun-dried tomatoes and the garlic and set aside. Beat together the vinegar, oil and chilli sauce, and season with salt and pepper. Peel and slice the peppers. Mix with the artichokes, tomatoes and garlic. Pour over the dressing and sprinkle with basil leaves.

Yogurt cheese in olive oil

Fills two 450g/1lb jars

In Greece, sheep's yogurt is drained and made into soft cheese, and here, little balls of cheese are bottled in olive oil with chilli and herbs. Try using garlic-infused oil for this recipe if you have it. Eat the cheese spread on lightly toasted bread.

800g/1³/₄lb Greek (US strained plain) sheep's yogurt
2.5ml/¹/₂ tsp salt
10ml/2 tsp crushed dried chillies
15ml/1 tbsp chopped fresh rosemary
15ml/1 tbsp chopped fresh thyme or oregano
about 300ml/¹/₂ pint/1¹/₄ cups olive oil

1 Sterilize a 30cm/12in square of muslin (cheesecloth) in boiling water and lay it over a plate. Mix the yogurt with the salt and tip it into the muslin. Bring up the sides of the muslin and tie with string. Hang it over a bowl to catch the whey and leave for 2–3 days in a cool place.

2 Sterilize two 450g/1lb jars by heating them in the oven at 150°C/300°F/Gas 2 for 15 minutes.

3 Mix together the dried chilli and herbs. Roll teaspoonfuls of the cheese into balls with your hands and lower into the jars, sprinkling each layer with the herb mixture.

4 Pour the oil over the cheeses to cover them completely, and store in the refrigerator for up to 3 weeks.

Variation
If the heat of chillies is not to your taste, try using fresh basil instead. You will need around 15ml/1 tbsp of fresh basil, torn into small pieces. This will make a lovely herby cheese. If you decide to leave out the other herbs, increase the amount of fresh basil you use accordingly.

Garlic prawns

Serves 4

Cook this simple Spanish tapas dish at the last minute, so you can take the prawns to the table still sizzling.

350–450g/12oz–1lb large raw prawns
(jumbo shrimp)
75ml/5 tbsp olive oil
2 red chillies, halved and deseeded
3 garlic cloves, crushed
salt and ground black pepper

1 Remove the heads and shells from the prawns, leaving the tails intact. Heat the oil in a flameproof pan suitable for serving.

2 Add the prawns, chillies and garlic to the pan and cook over a high heat for 3 minutes, stirring, until the prawns turn pink. Season lightly with salt and pepper and serve immediately.

Chorizo in olive oil

Serves 4

Spanish chorizo sausage is robustly seasoned with garlic, chilli and paprika. Serve this simple dish with bread to mop up the flavoured oil.

75ml/5 tbsp olive oil
350g/12oz chorizo sausage, sliced
1 large onion, thinly sliced
roughly chopped flat leaf parsley,
to garnish

1 Heat the oil and fry the chorizo over a high heat until beginning to colour. Remove from the pan with a slotted spoon.

2 Add the onion to the pan and fry until coloured. Return the chorizo to the pan for 1 minute to heat through. Tip the mixture into a serving dish and sprinkle with parsley.

SUBSTANTIAL DISHES

You can add the distinctive flavour of olive oil to every part of a meal, using it in marinades and dressings, to roast meat, soften vegetables for soups and stews and create luscious sauces. It is a perfect match for all the intense flavours of Mediterranean food.

Marinated red mullet with onion, pepper and aubergine

Serves 6

7.5ml/1^1/$_2$ tsp mild pimentón
45ml/3 tbsp flour
120ml/4fl oz/^{1}/$_2$ cup olive oil
6 red mullet or snapper, filleted
2 aubergines (eggplant), sliced
2 red or yellow (bell) peppers, seeded and sliced
1 large red onion, thinly sliced
2 garlic cloves, sliced
15ml/1 tbsp sherry vinegar
juice of 1 lemon
brown sugar, to taste
15ml/1 tbsp chopped fresh oregano
18–24 black olives
45ml/3 tbsp chopped fresh flat leaf parsley
salt and ground black pepper

This recipe is based on the Spanish method of cooking fish en escabeche – frying it then marinating it. Smoked paprika, known as pimentón, gives an authentic Spanish flavour.

1 Mix 5ml/1 tsp of the pimentón with the flour and season with salt and pepper. Heat half the oil in a large pan. Coat the fish in the flour and fry for 4–5 minutes until browned. Place in a non-metallic dish. Add another 30ml/2 tbsp of the oil to the pan and fry the aubergines until soft and browned. Add to the fish.

2 Add another 30ml/2 tbsp oil to the pan and soften the peppers and onion. Add the garlic and remaining pimentón and cook for a further 2 minutes. Stir in the vinegar and lemon juice with 30ml/2 tbsp water and bring to a simmer. Season with sugar to taste and add the oregano and olives.

3 Spoon the marinade over the fish. When cool, cover and leave in the refrigerator for several hours. Before serving, bring the dish back to room temperature and stir in the parsley.

Bouillabaisse

Perhaps the most famous of all Mediterranean fish soups, this recipe from Marseilles is a rich, colourful mixture of fish and shellfish, flavoured with olive oil, tomatoes, saffron and orange.

1.5kg/3–3¹/₂lb mixed fish and raw
shellfish, such as red mullet, John Dory,
monkfish, red snapper, whiting, large
prawns (shrimp) and clams
pinch of saffron strands
90ml/6 tbsp olive oil
1 onion, sliced
1 leek, sliced
1 celery stick, sliced
225g/8oz well-flavoured tomatoes,
peeled, seeded and chopped
2 garlic cloves, crushed
1 bouquet garni
1 strip pared orange rind
2.5ml/¹/₂ tsp fennel seeds
15ml/1 tbsp tomato purée (paste)
10ml/2 tsp Pernod
4–6 thick slices French bread
45ml/3 tbsp chopped fresh parsley
salt and ground black pepper

1 Remove the heads, tails and fins from the fish and put them in a pan with 1.2 litres/2 pints/5 cups water. Simmer for 15 minutes, then strain, reserving the liquid. Cut the fish into large chunks. Leave the shellfish in their shells. Soak the saffron in 15–30ml/1–2 tbsp hot water.

2 Heat the oil in a large pan and cook the onion, leek and celery until soft. Add the tomatoes, garlic, bouquet garni, orange rind and fennel seeds, then stir in the saffron and liquid, and the fish stock. Season, bring to the boil and simmer for 30–40 minutes.

3 Add the fish and boil for 5–6 minutes, until almost cooked. Add the shellfish and boil for a further 2 minutes. Lift out all the fish using a slotted spoon and transfer to a warmed serving dish.

4 Keeping the soup boiling, add the tomato purée and Pernod and check the seasoning. To serve, place a slice of French bread in each soup bowl and pour the broth over the top. Serve the fish separately, sprinkled with parsley.

Eliche with pesto

Serves 4

Pesto is traditionally made using a mortar and pestle, but a food processor is much easier. If you have a glut of fresh basil make a larger amount of pesto for freezing, but do not add the cheese until you use the sauce.

50g/2oz/1¹/₃ cups fresh basil leaves, plus a few leaves to garnish

2–4 garlic cloves

60ml/4 tbsp pine nuts

120ml/4fl oz/¹/₂ cup olive oil

115g/4oz/1¹/₃ cups freshly grated Parmesan cheese, plus extra to serve

25g/1oz/¹/₃ cup grated Pecorino cheese

400g/14oz/3¹/₂ cups dried eliche

salt and freshly ground black pepper

1 Put the basil, garlic and pine nuts in a blender or food processor and add 60ml/4 tbsp of the olive oil. Process until the ingredients are finely chopped, then slowly pour in the remaining oil. Turn the mixture into a large bowl and stir in the grated cheese. Taste and season if necessary.

2 Cook the pasta for the time recommended on the packet. Stir 45ml/3 tbsp of the pasta cooking water into the pesto in the bowl. Drain the pasta, then add to the bowl and toss well. Serve immediately, garnished with fresh basil leaves and accompanied by Parmesan.

Spaghettini with roasted garlic and oil

Olive oil plays a major role in this classic, simple pasta sauce, so use an oil with a distinctive flavour. Roasting the garlic makes it sweet and mild.

1 Preheat the oven to 180°C/350°F/Gas 4. Roast the garlic in an oiled baking tin (pan) for 30 minutes. When cool enough to handle, slice off the top third and dig out the flesh from each clove using the point of a knife. Add the oil and plenty of black pepper, and mix well.

2 Cook the pasta for the time recommended on the packet, drain it and return to the pan. Pour in the oil and garlic mixture and toss the pasta well over a low heat. Serve immediately with shavings of Parmesan.

Serves 4

1 whole head of garlic
120ml/4fl oz/$^1/_2$ cup olive oil
400g/14oz fresh or dried spaghettini
salt and freshly ground black pepper
coarsely shaved Parmesan cheese,
to serve

Rabbit salmorejo

This light, spicy sauté from Spain uses joints of rabbit, marinated for extra flavour. Rabbit is a very lean meat, and the large amount of olive oil will tenderize the meat.

1 Put the rabbit in a bowl with the wine, vinegar, oregano and bay leaves and toss together lightly. Cover the bowl and leave to marinate for several hours or overnight.

2 Heat the oil in a large pan. Drain the rabbit, reserving the marinade, and pat dry on kitchen paper. Fry on all sides until golden, then remove with a slotted spoon. Fry the onions until beginning to colour.

3 Remove the onions from the pan and add the chilli, garlic and paprika. Cook, stirring, for about a minute. Add the reserved marinade and the stock and season lightly.

4 Return the rabbit and the onions to the pan, bring to the boil then reduce the heat and simmer, covered, for about 45 minutes, until the rabbit is tender. Alternatively, transfer the stew to an ovenproof dish and bake in the oven at 180°C/350°F/Gas 4 for an hour.

Variation
If you find it difficult to get hold of rabbit joints, then this dish can be made with chicken instead. Use drumstick, wing or leg joints rather than breast portions.

Serves 4–6

675g/1$\frac{1}{2}$lb rabbit joints
300ml/$\frac{1}{2}$ pint/1$\frac{1}{4}$ cups dry white wine
15ml/1 tbsp sherry vinegar
a few oregano sprigs
2 bay leaves
90ml/6 tbsp olive oil
175g/6oz baby (pearl) onions, peeled, left whole
1 red chilli, seeded and finely chopped
4 garlic cloves, sliced
10ml/2 tsp paprika
150ml/$\frac{1}{4}$ pint/$\frac{2}{3}$ cup chicken stock
salt and ground black pepper

Chicken roasted with Mediterranean vegetables

Serves 4

This is a delicious method of roasting a chicken, which also works well with guinea fowl. Choose a free-range bird, and if it is available, one that has been corn-fed, as this will help give an authentic French flavour.

1.75kg/4–4¹/₂lb roasting chicken,
150ml/¹/₄ pint/²/₃ cup olive oil
¹/₂ lemon
few sprigs of fresh thyme
450g/1lb small new potatoes
1 aubergine (eggplant), cut into 2.5cm/1in cubes
1 red (bell) pepper, seeded and quartered
1 fennel bulb, trimmed and quartered
8 large garlic cloves, unpeeled
coarse salt and ground black pepper

1 Preheat the oven to 200°C/400°F/Gas 6. Rub the chicken all over with most of the olive oil and season with pepper. Place the lemon half and thyme inside the bird and put the chicken breast-side down in a large roasting pan. Roast for about 30 minutes.

2 Remove the chicken from the oven and season with salt. Turn right-side up and baste with the pan juices. Surround the bird with the potatoes, rolling them in the pan juices, and return to the oven.

3 After 30 minutes, add the remaining vegetables and garlic, and drizzle with the remaining oil. Season with salt and pepper and cook for a further 30–50 minutes, basting and turning the vegetables occasionally.

4 To check that the chicken is cooked, push the tip of a sharp knife between the thigh and breast. If the juices run clear it is done. The vegetables should be tender and just beginning to brown. Serve straight from the pan, drizzling some of the delicious juices over each serving.

VEGETABLES AND ACCOMPANIMENTS

Olive oil's rich taste and lubricating character makes it ideal for flavouring vegetable dishes to make the most of their delicate taste. Use the best virgin olive oil and sea salt for the simplest salad dressing, swirl it into sauces just before serving, or drizzle it over steamed vegetables, and warm, crusty bread.

Pistou and courgette fritters

In southern France pistou is traditionally served stirred into vegetable soup, but it also makes a perfect accompaniment to these delicious fritters, another speciality of the region.

For the pistou:
15g/^{1}/$_2$oz basil leaves
4 garlic cloves, crushed
90g/3^1/$_2$oz/1 cup grated Parmesan
cheese
finely grated rind of 1 lemon
150ml/^{1}/$_4$ pint/^{2}/$_3$ cup olive oil

For the fritters:
450g/1lb courgettes (zucchini), grated
75g/3oz/^{2}/$_3$ cup flour
1 egg, separated
15ml/1 tbsp olive oil
salt and ground black pepper

1 To make the pistou, crush the basil and garlic with a mortar and pestle to a fairly fine paste. Transfer to a bowl and stir in the cheese and lemon rind. Gradually blend in the oil, then pour into a serving dish.

2 To make the fritters, put the grated courgettes in a sieve over a bowl and sprinkle with plenty of salt. Leave to drain for 1 hour then rinse and dry on kitchen paper.

3 Sift the flour into a bowl and make a well in the centre. Add the egg yolk and oil. Measure 75ml/5 tbsp water. Whisk the egg yolk and oil, gradually incorporating the flour and water to make a smooth batter. Season and leave for 30 minutes. Stir the courgettes into the batter. Whisk the egg white until stiff, then fold into the batter.

4 Heat 1cm/^{1}/$_2$in of oil in a frying pan. Add dessertspoons of batter and fry for 2 minutes until golden. Drain the fritters on kitchen paper and keep warm while frying the rest. Serve with the pistou.

Lentil and spinach salad

This wonderful, earthy salad is great with robust barbecued food. It improves with standing and is best served at room temperature.

1 Make the dressing by whisking together all the ingredients. Drain the lentils and turn them into a bowl. Add most of the dressing and toss well, then set aside.

2 Heat the oil in a deep frying pan and cook the onion gently for 5 minutes until beginning to soften. Add the cumin and cook for 1 minute. Add the spinach, cover and cook until wilted, stirring occasionally. Season to taste.

3 Stir the spinach into the lentils with the remaining dressing and chopped parsley. Adjust the seasoning, before serving with French bread.

Serves 4

225g/8oz/1 cup Puy lentils, cooked with bouquet garni
30ml/2 tbsp olive oil
1 onion, finely chopped
10ml/2 tsp crushed toasted cumin seeds
400g/14oz young spinach
salt and ground black pepper
30–45ml/2–3 tbsp chopped fresh parsley

For the dressing:
75ml/5 tbsp olive oil
5ml/1 tsp Dijon mustard
15–25ml/3–5 tsp red wine vinegar
1 garlic clove, finely chopped

To serve:
thinly sliced French bread, toasted

Parsley and rocket salad with black olives and garlic dressing

Serves 6

Serve this light but distinctively flavoured salad as a well-rounded first course or as an accompaniment to rare roast beef.

1 garlic clove, halved
115g/4oz good white bread, sliced
45ml/3 tbsp olive oil, plus extra for frying
75g/3oz rocket (arugula) leaves
75g/3oz baby spinach
25g/1oz flat leaf parsley, leaves only
45ml/3 tbsp salted capers, rinsed and dried
40g/1¹/₂oz Parmesan cheese, shaved

For the dressing:
25ml/5 tsp black olive paste
1 garlic clove, finely chopped
5ml/1 tsp Dijon mustard
75ml/5 tbsp olive oil
10ml/2 tsp balsamic vinegar
ground black pepper

1 To make the dressing, whisk together the olive paste, garlic and mustard and gradually whisk in the oil, then the vinegar. Season to taste with pepper.

2 Heat the oven to 190°C/375°F/Gas 5. Rub the garlic clove over the bread and cut the slices into croutons. Toss them in the oil and bake on a baking tray for 10–15 minutes until golden brown.

3 Mix the rocket, spinach and parsley in a salad bowl. Heat some olive oil in a pan and fry the capers briefly until crisp. Drain on kitchen paper. Toss the dressing and croutons into the salad and scatter the Parmesan and capers over the top. Serve immediately.

Ratatouille

This versatile vegetable stew from Provence is a Mediterranean classic that is delicious hot or cold, alone or with eggs, fish or meat – it is a particularly good accompaniment to roast lamb.

1 Heat a little of the oil in a large, heavy pan and fry the onions for 5 minutes. Add the peppers and fry for a further 2 minutes. Remove the vegetables with a slotted spoon.

2 Add more oil to the pan and fry the aubergines for 5 minutes, then remove. Add the rest of the oil and fry the courgettes for 3 minutes, then remove them from the pan.

3 Add the tomatoes and garlic to the pan with the bay leaves and thyme. Season lightly and cook gently until the tomatoes have softened and are turning pulpy.

4 Return all the vegetables to the pan and cook gently, stirring frequently, for about 15 minutes. Season to taste. Drizzle with olive oil before serving.

120ml/4fl oz/¹/₂ cup olive oil, plus extra for drizzling
2 onions, thinly sliced
3 red or yellow (bell) peppers, seeded and cut into chunks
1 large aubergine (eggplant), cut into chunks
2 courgettes (zucchini), thickly sliced
900g/2lb ripe tomatoes, peeled, seeded and chopped
4 garlic cloves, crushed
2 bay leaves
15ml/1 tbsp chopped fresh thyme
salt and ground black pepper

Onion and anchovy pizza

Serves 6–8

This pizza is topped with ingredients introduced to Spain by the Moors, and still used today in many classic Spanish recipes.

400g/14oz/2¹/₂ cups strong white
bread flour
2.5ml/¹/₂ tsp salt
15g/¹/₂oz easy-blend (rapid rise) dried yeast
120ml/4fl oz/¹/₂ cup olive oil, plus extra
for frying
150ml/¹/₄ pint/²/₃ cup water
3 large onions, thinly sliced
50g/2oz can anchovies, chopped
30ml/2 tbsp pine nuts
30ml/2 tbsp sultanas (golden raisins)
salt and ground black pepper

1 Sift the flour and salt into a large bowl. Stir in the yeast, oil and water and mix to a dough. Turn out on to a floured surface and knead for about 10 minutes until smooth and elastic. Leave in an oiled bowl, covered, in a warm place for about an hour.

2 Preheat the oven to 240°C/475°F/Gas 9. Heat the extra oil in a frying pan and cook the onions until soft.

3 Knock back (punch down) the dough and roll out to a rectangle about 30 x 38cm/12 x 15in. Placed on an oiled baking sheet. Top with the onions, anchovies, pine nuts and sultanas. Season. Bake for 10–15 minutes and serve hot.

Index